· STOP THINKING ABOUT WRITING ·

...
JUST WRITE

· STOP THINKING ABOUT WRITING ·

JUST WRITE

· ALLISON DUKE ·

Stop Thinking About Writing . . . Just Write
Copyright © 2019 by Allison Duke
All rights reserved.
Published by PinkDreamInk.
Book design by Astrea Creative
Published in the United States of America

ISBN 978-1-7339737-0-0
05.07.19

TABLE OF CONTENTS

PREFACE	8
WRITE EVERY DAY	10
WRITE WITH A PLAN	22
WRITE IN PUBLIC	36
WRITE YOUR STORY	50
WRITE WELL	64
WRITE LIKE A NINJA	76
ACKNOWLEDGMENTS	91

For the Writers

PREFACE

Sounds like advice you should give yourself." These were the words of a friend when I presented my idea for this book and its title. My friend was right. Too often I call myself a writer but spend very little time actually writing. My list of publishing credits is practically nonexistent. I've written notebooks full of journals, an on-again off-again blog, a couple unfinished novels and a couple unpublished ones.

So, whether you're my friend or not, you might be wondering what credentials and experience I have to write this book. Here's what I've got: I'm a writer. I have been a writer for most of my life. I'm a creative who loves accomplishment and praise, and I am a chronic procrastinator. I put off the things I don't want to do until all I have time to do is the unpleasant things and not the things I want to do. I think that makes me the perfect person to write this book. I'm writing it for me. I'm writing it for you. And maybe I'm writing it for that friend of yours who keeps saying they want to write but rarely does it.

It's time. Get out your computer, your tablet, or some good old-fashioned tree-killing paper. Personally, I love writing in pink ink. Do what works for you, take this little guide along with you, and let's take some steps together on this journey. Let's do what we say we want to do. Let's be writers.

· WRITE EVERY DAY

> "The secret to your success is found in your daily routine."
>
> — *John C. Maxwell*

MAKE SUCCESS A HABIT

I'm starting out with a couple scary words here: Success. Habit. Do these words scare you? Do you welcome the thought of success, or is it a scary idea for you? Do your palms get sweaty at the idea of actually succeeding at something?

I have to admit, mine do. I've gone back and forth over the years wondering if I fear success or failure more. I do hate the idea of failure — public failure especially. That feeling of overwhelming shame and horror that trickles from the top of your head to your belly, making you want to run away while rooting you in place. Feeling hot and cold at the same time, and worst of all, helpless. It's a miserable feeling, and I've found that I can either avoid it altogether, or embrace it and stop worrying about it. I've spent the last 15 years or so developing an immunity to failure by failing at most of my endeavors.

In that time, I've learned something about failure: It's not nearly as scary as inaction. By failing, I learn. I learn how not to do that thing in the future, I do research so I can learn from the success of others, and sometimes I learn that doing that thing might not be a worthwhile use of my time. If I fail, at least I did something. It is a sort of accomplishment of its own. I learn nothing and accomplish nothing by sitting still, frozen in my fear of failure.

Almost as much as I fear failure, I fear success. I fluctuate between being lazy and driven, and my lazy side feels trepidation at the implications of success. Success inevitably means more work. More responsibility. More to keep up with. It may mean a change to my routine, and change exhausts me. This fear of success often keeps me from pursuing the goals I know I want to reach. Sometimes just the act of reaching for those goals requires uncomfortable stretching of my mind and comfort zone, so instead of reaching, I settle. I settle for the status quo, for what is good enough, for what might not even be working for me, because it's familiar and success is uncharted territory.

But if I never take those steps into what scares me, how many amazing things will I miss out on? The opportunities I have let pass me by haunt me. I wonder, what if I had actually done that thing I talked myself out of 10 years ago? Where would I be today? Where might I be in 10 years if I do what scares me today? Success might be scary, failure might be scarier, but we won't get anywhere unless we try. So let's try and create some habits that just might lead to success.

The very first step toward pursuing your interest in writing (I won't call it a passion yet, because maybe you haven't gotten that far) is deciding to do it. It doesn't matter now if you've ever written anything seriously before or only thought about it. You can start today. It doesn't matter if you're good at it or not. You can learn that. It doesn't even matter if you like

THE VERY
FIRST STEP
TOWARD
PURSUING
YOUR INTEREST
IN WRITING IS
DECIDING TO
DO IT

it or not. You'll find that out along the way. There are some days you won't like it, even if you decide that writing is your passion and calling. Loving something doesn't mean you will like it every day, but it does mean it's what you're meant to do, regardless of how you feel. It doesn't matter if you're successful or not. I can guarantee one way to fail, and that's to refuse to start. If you start, and keep going, and refuse to quit even if it's hard or uncomfortable or people don't support you, you will keep taking steps toward success, and right now that is what matters.

See, success isn't so scary, is it? Now let's talk about habits.

We create and break habits all the time, intentionally and unintentionally. If success truly lies in your daily routine, then you might need to create some intentional habits and a daily routine. I'm going to guess that if you're interested in writing, you have at least some creative aspect to your personality, and the idea of routine might be a bad word to you. It can feel that way for me. It brings up these horrible ideas of stifling boredom and sameness and … *blah*. I crave freedom and the ability to do what I want when I want to. And yet, I've found that my free spirit flourishes when I give it structure and familiarity and yes, even *rules*. I have very boring daily obligations that must be met, so I try to balance that with times when I can just relax and be me and let my creativity flow.

So I challenge you, if you've never done it before or even if you have, take a look at your daily activity. How are you spending your time? If one thing that keeps you from writing is never having enough time, where can you make some time?

Do you have pockets in your day that you can dedicate to writing? I encourage you to find that time every day. A full hour is always best for me but not always possible. If you can squeeze in half an hour to focus on writing when you wake up, or before you sleep, or at lunch, or after work, or any time in your day, do it. Plan to do it every day. Create the systems you need in order to put that plan in motion. Then, when it's time, sit down with your computer or your preferred writing tools and DO IT. Don't think, "Look at this free time I have. I should do some errands or chores or make a phone call or check social media or sleep..." NO! You will do those things with the other time you have. When you carve out writing time, use it for writing.

> Stop being a poser. Commit to being a writer.

Make a habit of it. Because if you don't, you are not a writer. You're a poser. That's right. I said it. Posers think about writing, and say they want to write, and join Facebook groups about writing, and read blogs about writing, but writers *write*. I want you to do something right now. Stop being a poser. Commit to being a writer.

Or stop reading this book. Actually, do exactly that. Stop reading this book right now and write something. It can be anything. A poem, a journal, a story, a rant about something that bothered you today, a personal manifesto, a love letter. It doesn't have to be good, it just has to be something. The more you do it, the easier it will be. Start your writing habit right now. Take a few minutes and write. Be a writer. And then come back and we'll take the next step.

Take action:
- **Write something.**
- **Evaluate your daily activity.**
- **Commit to write every day.**

FIND WHAT WORKS

Everyone is different. We all have personalities, families, life experiences, and circumstances that make us who we are today. You might be very different now than you were a few years ago, or you might have stayed essentially the same your entire life to this point. If you aren't at least a little bit familiar with who you are — what motivates you, what repels you, and what you value most in life — take some time to get to know yourself a little. Take some tests. StrengthsFinder, Myers-Briggs, and the Enneagram are popular and valuable tools. Pick one or more, take the tests, and think through the results. You need to know you in order to know what works for you.

You can also ask yourself a few questions. When is your mind the sharpest and most creative? When you wake up, after you shower, before you go to bed? Do you need absolute silence to work? Do you need an inspiring playlist blocking out the world around you? Can you work with others around, or do you require focused time with few interruptions? Can you write at home, or do you need to find a writing spot somewhere in your community?

Arm yourself with information about you, so you can combat those times when you need to write but inspiration doesn't come. Keep your identity and your purpose clear in your mind. Why do you write? Why are you writing what you're writing today? Are there other words you need to get out before you can focus on this project? Keep your goals, objectives, and most important, your purpose, in front of you so that you can confidently focus on your writing. What you write is part of who you are and reveals that truth to the world around you. You have something to contribute, a unique voice that no one else has. Share it.

Sometimes along the path to finding what works for you, you may stumble over what doesn't. This happened to me recently. I made a major change in my life: getting a part time job after years of being a stay-at-home mom. This required me to be much more intentional about when I do my daily writing. I had been living without a schedule or plan for using my time, and writing had become an occasional, "if I have time for it" kind of thing. That worked just fine before the part time job; now it wasn't working at all.

I created a daily schedule and found a time when I thought I would be able to focus on writing for at least half an hour. I thought I should have at least an hour between getting my kids to bed and getting myself to bed, so I plugged my writing time in there. On paper, it looked great. I added it to my calendar and put reminders in my phone.

After a week or two, I realized I hadn't actually used that

time to write. Not even once. The problem? With the part-time job on top of my already busy life, I was too mentally and physically spent to sit and write at the end of the day, even if I wanted to.

So instead of complaining that my plan wasn't working, I changed my plan. I decided to get up half an hour earlier in the morning to write. That way I could get it done, get my writing gears going, and have the option to write more as I had opportunities throughout the rest of the day. It also meant I could avoid feeling guilty and unfulfilled when I'd be so tired at the end of the day that I'd just fall into bed. Not only did it work, but I found on the first day that instead of dreading getting up and going to work, I was actually excited about getting up to to write. It helped me get out of bed and feel more alert and ready to start my day.

I plan to continue this morning writing whether or not I have a current project to work on. In *The Artist's Way,* bestselling author Julia Cameron presents a fascinating idea called morning pages. Strictly speaking, this is to be three pages of longhand, stream-of-consciousness writing, getting your thoughts on paper before you start your day. I have been trying this for a few months now, and I have to admit, I don't always give myself enough time to write three full pages. Still, the discipline of writing is valuable whether or not you follow someone else's "rules" to the letter.

Creating a plan is only one step toward creating the habit of writing. If you start your plan and find it doesn't work for you, you have permission to make adjustments and find what does work. Before giving up a plan, I do encourage you to really try it out first. In my above example, I kept my new schedule for several weeks before changing it. Most things about it did work. I just needed to find a better time to write. It can be tempting to give up on something before you've really put effort into it, especially if you're feeling nervous or uncertain about it. Don't give in to that temptation. Commit to make it work if you can, and work at it for awhile. Then if you know it really isn't for you, let it go and try something else.

In addition to finding a time that works for you, you need to find a place and a method. I can write at home in my favorite spot on the reclining couch with music playing in my ears, but my ideal place to write is always my local coffee shop. I love the atmosphere, the smell of coffee, the buzz of conversation, the people who come and go, the cars that drive by. There are probably writers who would find all that distracting, but I thrive on it. It's easier for me to write life into my words when there is life going on around me.

I write on a computer, in my favorite writing software, Scrivener. I am part of that "micro-generation" that grew up alongside computers. Personal computers weren't a thing when I was born, but by the time I was 10 I was familiar with word processing software. I wrote my first stories on lined paper, but I wrote my first "book" (which was about 10 chapters and about as many pages) on a computer.

I've tried to go back to writing on paper a few times because I love the idea of it, but I'm so reliant on removing and replacing large portions of text at one time (and moving them around as simply as I can in Scrivener) that I've reconciled myself to the fact that I am a computer writer. You might enjoy the simplicity of drafting on paper and then doing an automatic edit when you type your work in. You might be inspired by the sound and feel of a typewriter. You may write on a tablet or phone. What works for someone else might not work for you, and that's fine. You be you.

Take action:

Before you go on to the next section, take some time to think (and write) through these questions. Ask yourself:

- **Why do I write?**
- **What kind of person am I? What do I love most about life, people, activities, etc? What are my strengths?**
- **What do I write best?**
- **When is the best time to write?**
- **Where would I most love to write?**
- **What method do I use for writing?**

These answers may change for you over time and that's fine. You can always go back and revisit them later. For now, just get to know yourself enough that you have a starting place to move forward from.

WHAT WORKS FOR SOMEONE ELSE MIGHT NOT WORK FOR YOU, AND THAT'S FINE. YOU BE YOU.

STICK WITH IT

Now that you've created the habit of writing and discovered why you write and how you want to write, keep at it. "Write every day" is a simple concept, but speaking from experience, it's much more difficult in practice than it is on paper. What happens on the days when you don't want to get up in the morning, you're exhausted at the end of the day, or the time you set aside to write gets threatened by all those important, "real-life" things you have to do?

Stick with it. If you plan to write in the morning but you don't feel like getting up, remind yourself that you're a writer and that you have to get up and write. If your writing time is in the evening and you just want to go to bed, tell yourself to write for half an hour and then you can sleep. If your list of things to do tempts you to skip writing for today, add writing to your to-do list and get it done.

Life happens. We can set ourselves up for success, but we can't control everything. We get distracted and interrupted. Illnesses, vacations, and events disrupt our rhythm. We can always find reasons not to write, or at least to put it off for now, but let's not waste the work we've done to determine why we write, and let's give ourselves space to do it. Missing one day of writing might not seem to be a big deal, but what if I skip today and then something comes up tomorrow, and I find something else to do the day after that? That carefully crafted creature of habit is easy to destroy. Skipped days turn into weeks, and then we're back to thinking about writing and not actually doing it.

When it comes to pursuing any goal, including writing, we often get in our own way. It's important to deal with obstacles and objections and keep going, rather than getting sidelined by them. If you do need to step away from your writing for some reason, make yourself a promise that you will get back to it, preferably at a specific day and time. Set reminders, create accountability, take care of whatever it is that is pulling you away, and then come back.

The reason why I'm so dogmatic about this concept is that I know it works. Way back in November of 2011, I attempted National Novel Writing Month (NaNoWriMo, or just NaNo, for short). Never in my life had I been so disciplined and dedicated to writing for such a focused period of time. I didn't "win." I only wrote about half of the 50,000 words that is the goal for the month. But for me, it was a turning point. For the first time, I went from calling myself a writer to being a writer. Instead of talking and thinking about writing but only actually writing occasionally, I gave myself a real goal with a deadline and worked toward it. I *wrote.*

I learned important lessons about myself as a writer. I learned that when I'm focused I can write 1,000 words in an hour, and if I'm really in the zone I can write 1,500. I learned that action creates momentum, and that the more frequently I write, the easier it becomes to write. Words, scenes, and dialogue just start to flow. I also learned that for me, writing quickly can often mean writing badly, but it's better than writing nothing. Bad writing can be fixed but a blank page is just ... blank.

· STOP THINKING ABOUT WRITING...JUST WRITE ·

Some writers love NaNo and do it every year. They love the motivation, the tribe, the daily push to meet a certain word count every day. It can certainly be a great motivator for writers who tend to be lazy, waiting on their muse before they start writing. The business of writing means word count requirements and deadlines, so you might as well get used to the idea. For me, I find November to be a terrible time to write a novel. The stress and rush of the holiday season really kicks off in November, and it's hard for me to write a lot during that time. But then, is there any good time to write a novel? If we wait for the right time, we may wait forever. So I may do NaNo again, if it works out that I'm ready to start a novel and push through the first 50,000 words around that time of year. If you're a fiction writer and you've never done it, why not give it a try? Whether you win or not, the experience will be valuable.

> Bad writing can be fixed but a blank page is just ... blank.

How are you feeling now about your identity as a writer? Are you ready to get serious about this writing thing? The first step is simple. Create a habit of writing every day. Find out what has been stopping you, what works for you, and then just do it. Now. And again tomorrow. And every day, until it becomes such a part of you that you don't even have to tell people you're a writer anymore, because they'll know.

Take action:
- **Take at least 30 minutes and write whatever words are drifting around in your head, waiting to be written. Repeat this tomorrow, and the next day. Just write. Then continue to the next step: Write with a plan.**

· WRITE WITH A PLAN

"A goal without a plan is just a wish."

— *Antoine de Saint-Exupéry*

KNOW WHERE YOU'RE HEADED

I always like to approach life with a plan, so that I can then ignore it while reminding myself that at least I have one if I need it. That's my basic approach to writing, too. I love outlines. I have loved them since I first learned how to make them. I love how neat and tidy they look with all their indents and subsections. They are my go-to writing plan. I've used them forever, for every kind of writing I do. Outlining is a very important step of my writing process, whether I'm writing a novel, a research paper, a blog, or this book. If I have an outline, I have something to work from. It gives me confidence and a sense of accomplishment.

As much as I enjoy making outlines, I tend to ignore them once I start writing. This is particularly true of my fiction writing. I actually considered myself a "pantser" at one time. Are you familiar with that term? Writers often like to align themselves into one of two camps: Plotters and pantsers. Plotters like to have their plan in mind when they start writing, and pantsers write "from the seat of their pants." I'm a little bit of both. I do start with an outline, but often my finished work hardly resembles the original outline at all. The last time I started a novel, I outlined every scene when I started. Then as I wrote, I added scenes, took some out, moved some around, altered a whole plot point, added a character or two, and changed my ending several times. This is all ridiculously easy to do in Scrivener, which is only one of many reasons I love that program. It helps me embrace the strange hybrid plotter/pantser that I really am.

When setting out on a journey, it's important to know where you're going. It is perfectly acceptable to amble around with no real plan or purpose, discovering new places and things along the way. However, if your intention is to start in one place and get to another, you should have at least a general idea of how you're going to make that happen. If you're on a hike or a road trip or going somewhere for the first time, you need a map, or at least directions. If you're writing, you need an outline, or a cork board or a brainstorming bubble, or something that is leading you where you want to go.

A few years ago I stumbled upon K. M. Weiland, an author and blogger whose planning resources have helped me improve my writing process immensely. I particularly love her book (and accompanying workbook) Outlining Your Novel. Her outlining process is extremely intensive and detailed but also encourages flexibility and creativity. She also has excellent thoughts on character arc, plot and structure, and other writerly issues. It's worth your time to look her up.

When you write, know what you're writing. If you're giving instruction, outline your process. If you're teaching on a topic, get it organized. If you're writing a story, know the plot points and character arcs and how they will tie together. Start with the end in mind. When I wrote my first novel, I didn't decide how I wanted to end it until I got there. It was frustrating, trying to decide where the story should end. I realized in that process that my plot was weak, and that if I had a better plan, I could write a better story.

In my next novel, I had two possible endings. I didn't choose one until late in the writing process, but I knew I could write with both of them in mind. Once I got to that point, the writing I had already done pointed toward one ending as better than the other. I plan to write another novel once I finish this book, and I want to have the ending clear in my mind when I start. It helps bring continuity to the whole work.

Ultimately, it doesn't matter how you plan, as long as you do. When I start a new project, I begin on paper with a lengthy brainstorming and outlining process. Then I set up my outline in Scrivener. I don't start with chapters; I start with scenes and arrange them into chapters later. I have my beginning, middle, and end, and I place my scenes within those. I write a couple sentences to describe each scene.

To some of you, that may seem like a lot of detail and work in the planning process, and to others, it may not sound like enough. It works for me, especially since I've learned to unleash my creativity and come up with a great story in the pre-writing stage, before I ever get an actual word of dialogue or description typed into my book. If you have a different process that works for you, use that. If not, get some writing craft books, read some author blogs, pick a method, and give it a try. Make yourself a map before you start your writing journey. Some of the stops along the way may surprise you, but knowing your ultimate destination will help you keep your focus.

Take action:

Create some kind of outline or plan for your next writing project.

If you get stuck, ask yourself questions like:

- **What do I want to accomplish through this project?**
- **What are the main points I need to include?**
- **What can I add to make it more exciting, unexpected, emotional, or entertaining?**
- **Look up K. M. Weiland's outlining process or find one that works even better for you.**

BE WILLING TO TAKE DETOURS

As I mentioned earlier, one thing I like to do when I have a plan is to ignore it completely. If I'm being honest, which I usually am, my plans are almost always backup plans in case I get completely off-track. Like a safety net for when I jump off a cliff. I make a plan, and then I just write, letting my inner wild child run free. If I get lost or stuck, I come back to the plan and say, "Oh yeah … that's where I was going." Then I adjust. Life is less fun if you're so focused on where you're going that you miss the beauty along the way.

Planning is important, but the actual writing is much more important. It's when you write that your creativity really begins to flow. It may take you places you didn't expect

MAKE YOURSELF A MAP BEFORE YOU START YOUR WRITING JOURNEY.

> Life is less fun if you're so focused on where you're going that you miss the beauty along the way.

to go, and that's okay. Be willing to explore the side trails your mind takes you on. You may get lost and have to retrace your steps, but you might also find new adventures you never expected.

In writing fiction, I have occasionally created characters specifically so I could kill them. I do this so that I'm less emotionally attached when the time comes for them to die. It's just one of those senselessly cruel things writers do sometimes. Once, however, a character I created for that purpose really came to life and won me over in just a few scenes. Then when it came time to kill him off, I couldn't do it. Instead I created an entire new purpose for that character and made him an integral part of my story. Things like that don't always work. I have to admit, there were a few times when I thought, "I should have just killed this guy when I was supposed to. It would have been easier." But ultimately, I think the story was better because let I him live.

I like to start my books with every scene planned out, but I add and remove scenes along the way. I think it's easier to have that freedom when I already know where I'm going with the story. As I write it, I might find that one scene I planned is unnecessary or in the wrong place. Or maybe one particular plot point takes more scenes to develop than I had expected. Once I added five scenes between one scene and the scene I had originally thought would come next.

Because I take the time before I start writing to plan out my story, my mind often keeps me closer to the outline than I realize. In my last book, even with all my alterations along the way, I hit half of my expected word count almost exactly halfway through my outline. That was a good feeling. As writers we have incredible freedom not only to create, but to explore and expand our creations along the way. We'll talk later about writing elegantly and crafting concise language, but in your initial drafts, just give your imagination freedom to run wild. You can always rein it in later.

Don't be afraid to get caught up in your writing and let your mind take you into new territory. A lot of writers tend to write the same things over and over. I've written almost the exact same scene, with completely different characters, in at least two books. I'm talking almost verbatim, with dialogue and everything, and I didn't do it intentionally. A favorite author of mine growing up repeated the same storyline in at least four different fiction series. It didn't deter me from reading his books, but I remember thinking, "Oh, we're doing this one again? Really?" If you always stick to the same plan or formula for writing, you may get repetitive. Ask yourself new questions. Explore new approaches to a scene or character. Try something you've never done before. Even better, try something you refuse to do.

For years I avoided first-person present tense because I find it difficult to read and even more difficult to write. Although that style works for some genres, being in the main character's head as the action unfolds, it's easy for authors to slip back into a more traditional narrative voice. In the planning stages of my last novel, when I was considering the approach I was taking and the challenges my character had to overcome, I realized that first-person present tense would convey those thoughts and feelings better than any other approach. I complained bitterly about it for a week or two. Some friends just shrugged and said, "Don't write it that way if you don't want to. It's your book." They were right, of course, but I decided I should at least try it. I wrote that entire novel in first-person present. It was just as difficult as I expected it to be, but by the end I started feeling comfortable with it. I don't know if I'll ever write another book that way, but at least I know now that I can.

If the idea of trekking off into new writing territory makes you nervous, remember that you have a plan. If you veer off too far and don't like the direction you're heading, abandon that idea or thought trail and come back to the plan. No writing is ever wasted, even if it never sees the light of day. It's just practice, and we all need more of that. We don't get better at writing by thinking about writing, or even by reading about writing. We improve with practice. At the end of the day, it's better to write something that ends up in the trash than to not write anything at all.

NO WRITING IS EVER WASTED, EVEN IF IT NEVER SEES THE LIGHT OF DAY.

Take action:
- **Take a few minutes to plan out a short fiction scene, blog post, or a section of an instructional or reflective work.**
- **Write at least 1,000 words. Look back at the plan, or don't. Just practice writing.**

DON'T LOSE SIGHT OF THE GOAL

We all have a purpose in writing. If you've been following the action steps, you should have at least a fuzzy idea of why you write and where you want to go with your writing. I used to say, "I don't care if it gets published or not, as long as a few people read it and enjoy it." That is still true about all my writing. Except for my journal, which I only write for me, I write for others to read. Ultimately however, my dream is much bigger than that. I want to write award-winning fiction. I admit, it's a lofty goal, but I've kept it close to my heart. That vision compels me not only to write, but to keep getting better at it—to refine my skills and come to the point where the characters leap off the page and into readers' hearts through beautifully concise language. It also means that someday I'm going to have to release my fiction to the world, allowing it to be enjoyed but also criticized, rejected but also published. Sometimes it's scary having a goal. It's easy to give in to self-doubt and say, "No, I just write for myself, because I have to get words out, not because I want anyone to read it." Giving in to doubt and fear will not get me anywhere. Digging in, doing the hard thing, saying the scary words so other people ask me how it's going and keep me accountable will move me forward, in the direction I know I want to go.

Is your goal big? Does it scare you? If so, good. If not, that's okay too. You don't have to have a big scary goal, but you have to have a goal. Once you have it clear in your mind, keep it in front of you. Write it down. Talk about it. You don't have to make it the topic of every conversation (because soon most people won't want to talk to you) but mention it. Elaborate if people ask. Don't hide your dreams in your heart. Get them out there. Some people won't understand, some might laugh, but some will encourage you along the way and a few might even help you.

I write my dreams in pink ink. Those pink letters encourage me to keep learning, keep growing, keep working. PinkDreamInk is so important to me that I made it into a brand and adopted it into my image. Anyone who knows me at all knows that it's a part of who I am. What about you? Are your dreams hidden away in a dusty corner of your life, or have you put them out for people to see? Don't let fear keep them hidden. Bring them out, dust them off, breathe life into them, and see what happens next.

The best way to achieve any goal is to break it down into manageable steps. When my schedule was extremely fluid, it was difficult for me to deal with daily steps, so I broke down my goals weekly. In writing terms, this usually meant writing a certain number of words per week or editing a certain number of scenes. If I didn't accomplish what I needed to by

Saturday, I knew I had work to do. I still have weekly goals, but now that my schedule is more fixed, it's easier for me to break projects down into daily steps. I feel a sense of relief and accomplishment when I meet my daily word count goal. It makes me feel like I've done my job. I can keep writing if I have time or move on to other things, but I have done what I needed to do as a writer. That is a good feeling.

In some ways, an outline or writing plan is like a goal. If you have a plan and you know what you're working toward, you can track your progress as you get there. Even if you deviate from the plan, it's still there, keeping you accountable, reminding you of your ultimate destination. You can break down your plan and get a good idea for how many scenes or chapters or words you need to write every day or every week in order to meet your deadline. If this sounds too structured for you, if all your feelings resist the idea of boxing yourself in like that, I encourage you to try it anyway. If you find after a month or two that it does, in fact, stifle your writing, you can go back to exercising your creativity freely and without restraint. More power to you. If you're anything like me, however, you may find that a little planning on the front end can help you sustain your vision and get to your ending. It's worth the effort.

Take action:
- **What is your writing goal or dream? Write it down.**
- **Keep your goal and your writing plan in front of you when you write.**

· WRITE WITH A PLAN ·

When you wander from your plan and lose track of where you want to be, come back and let it remind you where you were going.

· WRITE IN PUBLIC

"Just write poorly.

Continue to write poorly,

in public, until

you can write better."

— *Seth Godin*

GET YOUR WORDS OUT THERE

Up until this point we've been doing very quiet, private work. Motivation, consistency, and planning are things you can do completely on your own. You can tell others about it but you don't have to. Writers tend to be introverts so my guess is, you probably haven't said much to anyone. We could go along in our quiet lives, doing our quiet work, or we can take the next step. It can be a challenge, but it's important: Write in public.

And no, I don't just mean sitting at a coffee shop, visible but still in relative anonymity, typing away or scrawling in notebooks. Although that is my preferred environment for writing, what I'm talking about is taking the next step away from just thinking about writing, into embracing your identity as a writer. Write words that other people can read. Put them out in public, where people can see them, appreciate them, and criticize them. You may think of yourself as a writer, but it will change your world when other people start thinking of you that way, too. The only way for that to happen is for you to allow others to read what you write.

Our world today is so full of opportunities to write publicly, there is no excuse not to. We live in the age of the internet and social media, where expressing yourself in a public setting is only as difficult as a tweet, Instagram, status update, or blog post. Pick a public medium and start writing. You can write on Facebook if you feel safer posting so only friends and family can see it, but I prefer something more public than that. On Twitter, you must express your thoughts in 280 characters or less. I find that that is enough for a complete, fully developed thought, including hashtags and usually without abbreviations. It was a little more difficult back when the limit was 140 characters, but still possible. You can also start a blog and write several paragraphs on your chosen topic. If the thought of people reading and commenting on your writing makes you sick to your stomach, you can turn off comments. If you choose to write on Twitter, I'd recommend tweeting at least once a day. If you blog, once a week is usually enough.

Other ways to write publicly include freelance writing, posting stories in author forums, joining a community writing group, or even commenting regularly on someone else's writing blog. Whatever you choose, commit to be consistent. You will discover and hone your voice through public interaction even faster than by writing in secret.

Don't worry about writing perfectly. There will always be critics, people who think your writing is trash, people who think they can write better. Most of those people aren't actually writing, beyond their negative comments and overcritical reviews.

I learned this concept years ago from Seth Godin's blog and it has changed my thoughts about writing words people might actually read immediately. It's okay if you don't write well, especially at first. You'll get better, and we'll talk later about ways to do that. In some venues you can even go back and edit yourself if you see a mistake or think of a way to word something better. What's important is practice. Public practice. If you're used to getting feedback on your writing, the idea of presenting it to an agent, editor, or client should be somewhat less daunting. If it's not absolutely terrifying, if you can think to yourself, "Well, so-and-so said such-and-such about my writing and I didn't die, so this won't be so bad," then you may be more likely to submit when that time comes. And who knows? Maybe by then the person you're submitting to might have already heard of you!

Take action:
- **Pick a public venue for your writing.**
- **Write something and put it out there for other people to see.**

GROW YOUR TRIBE

As you write more and more publicly, you will begin to gather some people who relate to your words and your voice. You may have friends and family who read what you write simply because they love you. You may be involved with groups in your community who will relate to your writing. There will be others you may not even know yet, who appreciate what you have to say and how you say it. You may connect with other writers through a variety of methods and circumstances. You may find a niche among people who love the same things you do. There are some people who call this growing a platform or an audience, and those are both good words. I prefer another popular term for this process: growing your tribe.

A tribe is like a family. It is made up of people who may have diverse backgrounds, ages, genders, ethics, worldviews, and perspectives on life, but they all have at least one thing in common: They are your people. They read what you write. They may be your family, friends, people you've met online, people you know only through writing, etc. In a few cases they might be people you don't really like, but if they read and enjoy what you write, they are valuable members of your tribe.

I am not *exactly* a people person. I usually fall into the middle of the introvert/extrovert scale. I love being with people but I'm also a bit antisocial and I don't like parties or crowds. However, I am *definitely* a relationship person. I love getting to know people and building relationships. I absolutely believe that the people in my life are my greatest asset. Wealth, security, and success are hollow wins without people to share all that with. I never want to mow people down on my way to success. I want to take them with me. So this idea of a tribe of people all sharing life's journey together really appeals to me.

Your tribe will become invaluable during your writing process. They will be your first readers, your free editors and proofreaders, your sounding boards, and your cheerleaders. Sometimes they may even be your harshest critics, whose words haunt you and compel you to write better and overcome obstacles on your path to success. They keep you accountable whether or not you ask them to. In those times when writing is the last thing you want to do, someone in your tribe will ask, "How's your book going?" or "Have you blogged lately?"

Once you give your words wings and send them out into the world, your tribe will be the jet stream that carries them farther than you can yourself. If your books are published traditionally, they will buy them enthusiastically and send you pictures of them on the shelf. If you go the self-published route, they will post about your books on social media and review them on retail sites. They will read and comment on your blog, and possibly share it with others. They will do marketing for you because they love you and what you have to say, and you can't put a price on that.

Your tribe may start out small, only 20 people or so, or if you are an influencer your tribe may already be very large. Either way you should seek to grow your tribe whenever you can, outside of your writing time. Do this in a genuine way. If you annoy people, particularly online, you may lose them. If people like you, it's because of you, not because of your constant marketing presence. Learn how to market well. Even if you're published by the biggest publishers and offered the most lucrative contracts, you still have to market yourself to people. Invite them to like your status, comment on your blog, buy your book, come to a signing, follow your board, quote your tweets, whatever it takes. But do it as a natural process of getting to know people, not as a constant commercial. People want to feel like they know you. They don't want to feel like you only care about what you're trying to sell them.

I know almost nothing about marketing. I don't have a degree, I've never worked in the field, I haven't done much of it beyond selling cosmetics in a direct sales environment, and I was only ever moderately successful at that. But I'm writing this book and you're reading it and we're talking about marketing, so here's a tip: Think about what approaches attract you, and use those. Then think about the approaches that annoy you, and (you guessed it) don't use those. Here are a few things that suck me in:

- Facebook videos with captions. I rarely watch videos with the sound on. If I really like a video I might turn on the sound and watch it again. If a video doesn't have captions, I probably won't watch it. The exceptions are food videos and dog videos. I almost always watch those whether they have captions or not.
- Pins with pretty pictures and nice fonts.
- Blogs with pretty pictures and nice fonts.
- Really anything with pretty pictures and nice fonts.
- User-Friendly, mobile-friendly websites.
- Puppies, unicorns, butterflies, and rainbows. I'm not even kidding.
- Clever use of language.
- Limited, relevant hashtags.
- Personal interaction.

I am very likely to spend money on anything that uses at least one of these approaches. And I'm extremely unlikely to

ONCE YOU GIVE YOUR WORDS WINGS AND SEND THEM OUT INTO THE WORLD, YOUR TRIBE WILL BE THE JET STREAM THAT CARRIES THEM FARTHER THAN YOU CAN YOURSELF.

spend money if I see one of the following annoying things:
- Facebook Live videos. Most of these are painful to watch, so I don't. And there are no captions. Also the sound starts playing as soon as you click on it and that can be bad.
- Pins that are the wrong format.
- Blogs that have frequent, excessive typos. I can forgive a few, but more than two or three is too much.
- Ads with typos or grammatical errors.
- Direct messages asking me to buy something.
- Twitter accounts that are entirely self-promotion.
- Excessive hashtags, or more than three or four.
- Spiders or blood.

These are just my lists. You may have your own. Some of the things that bother me might be some of the things that attract you. Take some time to think through what works for you and what doesn't. If you use an approach that draws you in, you just might be able to use it to attract people like you. Most of us are writing for people who are like us. We want diverse audiences, and many different people might connect with you on different levels, but they are connecting with *you*, what you like and who you are. Use that.

Offering people what they want and letting them know why they want it is one of the basic tenets of sales. Sales and marketing are not dirty words. We all buy and sell every day. The key is to make sure you sell the right way to the right people. Even if some expert swears by some approach that made them a fortune, if you don't like it, you probably won't have the same level of success. However, you won't have any level of success if you don't get out there and grow your tribe.

Take action:
- **Think about your current tribe. How big is it? How well do you know your people, and how well do they know you?**
- **What are some ways you can grow your tribe?**
- **Write down a list of places, real and online, where you can find more people.**
- **What are your current marketing do's and don'ts?**

GET COMFORTABLE WITH DISCOMFORT

Ah, comfort. We seek it out in our houses, our relationships, our food. Comfort is an old friend, a warm blanket, a relaxing soak at the end of a long day. It goes hand in hand with security and often is one of the most important things in our lives. It can be so important to us that we choose it at our own expense, whether it costs us time, money, effort, or even success.

Some success gurus out there preach that comfort is the great enemy, that success always lies outside our comfort zones, that comfort should be abandoned in the pursuit of excellence. However, for many of us, comfort is the desired object of our lives. So does it really make sense to abandon it in order to achieve it?

Sometimes.

Have you ever known someone you could describe as too comfortable? Someone who could do more, become more, possibly achieve great things, but who has settled for good enough? Maybe they don't want to try harder, maybe they are afraid to. They come up with excuses for why they can't or won't do something when the simple fact is they're comfortable where they are and don't consider change to be a worthwhile effort. Comfortable people can be frustrating to work with or sometimes even live with because they often resist change, even necessary change. Maybe this describes someone you know or love. Maybe it describes you.

> Comfort is not the enemy of success. It can be our motivation for success.

I tend to look at many things in life from a moderate viewpoint, and comfort is one of those things. I love my comfort zone. There are few things I enjoy more than curling up in my spot on the couch with a blanket, a favorite beverage, and a book, game, or movie. While I am writing this, I am in that spot with my blanket and my coffee, enjoying one of my favorite activities. I am comfortable. However, in order to get into this spot I had to get up earlier than I wanted to, make the coffee, force myself to stop playing a game on my phone and researching a product on the internet, and write. If I'd decided to just stay in my comfortable warm bed,

I wouldn't be writing this right now. Sometimes we do have to give up a little bit of comfort in order to gain what we really want.

Comfort is not the enemy of success. It can be our motivation for success. But along that path, we may find that we need to give up some momentary comforts in order to clear the path that leads to what we really want. So take a look at what might be holding you back from writing. How many of those things are within your control? Focus your efforts on changing what you can control and change, because it's a waste of time and mental energy to fret about what you can't. Do you need to make a mindset adjustment, or find a new environment to write in, or maybe give up one hobby or activity in your life in order to dedicate more time to writing? Well then, do it.

Next, consider what you have refused to do in the past. Fill in the blank: "I'm not a _____ person." Why not? What is your reason for not doing something? Is it a legitimate reason, or just stubbornness? Sometimes if you choose to do that thing you don't do, you find something you've been needing to do for a long time. In the past few years I've started challenging myself to take on some of those things I've always refused to do. I already mentioned writing an entire novel in first-person present tense when for years I said, "Oh, I don't do that." Once, I did planks every day for a month. I did burpees every day for a week. I added push-ups and jumping jacks to my daily workout. I made Rice Krispie treats, and they were delicious. I made pie, and pizza, and lasagna, and pretty cakes. I got on Pinterest, and that certainly changed my life. I even joined Planet Fitness after swearing for years I would never join a gym and laughing at anyone who suggested it. We get so comfortable with all the things we say no to. I'm not suggesting that you say yes to everything. But maybe, every once in awhile, say yes to something.

Trying new things is uncomfortable. Putting myself out there is uncomfortable. Every time my finger hovers over the "Publish" button on my blog, I think, "Do I really want to do this?" Sometimes I don't want to, but I do it anyway. Prepping a manuscript for submission, then actually submitting it, is so terrifying that I still haven't done it. But I will. I'm working on it, and when it's ready, I will do it. Even if I write award-worthy fiction, it will never actually win any awards if I keep it locked away in a file on my computer. I have to take that scary, uncomfortable step if I ever want to have any real hope of seeing my dreams come true. And so do you.

Just like I've embraced failure as a step toward success, I've also embraced discomfort as a necessary part of the pursuit of my dreams. I've known people who simply told me they were comfortable with who they were and the life they lived, and there's nothing wrong with that. Contentment is a valuable quality. But if you dream of being something more than what you are today, you must get comfortable with discomfort. Take a step outside your comfort zone, and then another, and another, and soon you may find yourself traveling the road toward your dreams.

Take action:
- List some things you've refused to do in the past, and why.
- Pick at least one of those things that you will do today or tomorrow.
- Commit to becoming comfortable with discomfort.
- Write something.

· WRITE YOUR STORY

"Today you are You,

that is truer than true.

There is no one alive

who is Youer than You."

— *Dr. Seuss, Happy Birthday to You!*

WRITE WHAT YOU WANT TO READ

Now that we've gone through some of the motivational process of writing, it's time to get a little more practical. So … what are you going to write? To help answer that question, I have two more questions for you. What do you want to write? Is there a subject that you're passionate about, or a story that has been developing in your imagination? If so, the answer to your question is fairly obvious. Write about that subject. Bring your expertise and perspective to it. Write that story you've always wanted to write. It's hanging around in your head for a reason. Let it out.

What if you have a burning passion to write, but you can't think of anything worth writing? Writer's block is real, but it's not a valid reason to stop writing or to wait to start. It's an obstacle that any real writer should be able to get around. It takes discipline and intentional thinking, but it is possible. Try looking at your work from another perspective. Take another angle on your topic. Write a scene from a different character's point of view. If you're stuck on one project, work on something else. What do you like to read about? What are your favorite nonfiction topics? What are your favorite books? Do you ever think, "I wish someone would write a book about…" Grant your own wish and write that book!

Some writers and publishers talk a lot about following trends, writing what is selling right now, getting on the money train. If you haven't noticed this before, you will now. A fresh, new book, different in some way from what everyone has been reading, will hit the market and sell like crazy. For a few years, there will be dozens of books whose covers or reviews proclaim them to be "the next" of that popular book or series. The next Harry Potter. The next Hunger Games. The next book everyone is talking about. Everyone wants to write or publish the next great bestseller, and what better way to determine what will sell than to look at what is selling now, right? Maybe.

In traditional publishing, which is still the best path to producing a bestseller, it takes approximately a year to take a book from an accepted manuscript to the shelves, whether they be physical or virtual. So let's say you look at what's selling now and decide to write something similar to that. Suppose it takes you a year to write your book, polish it to perfection, and send it off to agents and acquisitions editors, or pitch it to them at conferences. After several rejections and rewrites, your dream comes true and your manuscript sells. In this scenario it takes about three years for your book to go from a vague concept to a physical reality. Are you willing to bet that the same kinds of books that are flying off the shelves right now will still have that level of appeal in three years? I'm not. Some genres have a lot of staying power, but for the most part, three years from now people will be ready for something fresh and different. If you write your story, regardless of what is selling right now, you might just be that fresh and different voice that readers are ready for.

Of course, self-publishing can move much faster. If you really want to get in on what is popular today, you can take a course on how to write fast, find out what's trending, write a book in a month or two, hire some freelancers to edit it, and get it out there in six months or less. People have done that and been successful, so I'm not going to say it doesn't work. If you want to write for small, immediate profit, that might be a good strategy for you. Personally though, I think you will find your writing experience to be much more satisfying if you take the time to think through and write the stories or topics that capture your heart and mind and won't let go.

My favorite genre is fantasy. I'm talking old-school, world-hopping, magic quests and mythical creatures fantasy. People in publishing often say that fantasy is dead, that no one reads it and no one buys it, so you're better off writing something else. But is that really true? Fantasy is the mother genre of dozens of series that are selling really well these days. Paranormal romance, alternative history, mythological adventures, steampunk, post-apocalyptic worlds where people develop mental powers, and schools of witchcraft and wizardry all fall into subgenres of fantasy. And if that's not enough, one of the most popular book and TV series at this writing, Game of Thrones, is high fantasy at its darkest. Fantasy is not dead. It is very much alive, and I think it always will be. People long for adventure stories that take them away from reality while grounding them in some universal themes, and fantasy is one of the best ways to do that. So I'm confident that when I'm ready to sell fantasy, there will be an audience to buy it. That's only one example.

Market is important, and when it comes time to pitch your work, you'll want to have something popular to compare it to. But let that drive your marketing, not your writing. Don't write for the trends. Write for you. If you write the best, truest story you can write, there will probably be people who will want to read it. If not, call that a practice book and write something else. No effort is wasted in this writing life.

The world doesn't need the next bestseller in an oversaturated market. The world needs stories. Whether you write fiction or nonfiction, tell stories. Tell the stories you want to read. You never know; maybe someone else will want to read them, too.

Take action:
- **List some stories you've always wanted to write or topics that you're passionate about.**
- **Pick two or three from your list that stand out to you and develop them with your favorite brainstorming method.**
- **Write at least 500 words.**

WRITE WHAT YOU KNOW

"Write what you know" is a piece of writing advice that I've heard so many times, I don't know the original source for it. But what does it actually mean? Taking the statement at face value, it sounds as though it could severely limit an author's options when it comes to the type and scope of story or information to write about. In this strange age, many people on the internet have declared that you can only speak or write or voice an opinion on a certain topic or idea if you have real, personal experience with it.

Authors (and readers) look at an idea like that and roll their eyes, because we know that many of the world's greatest books would not have been written if writers had not dared to look beyond themselves and write characters and stories that are far from their personal experiences. Not everything has to be autobiographical. Everything we write is shaped by our worldview and what we've lived, but we are truly only limited by the scope of our imaginations and the amount of information available to us.

So if writing what you know doesn't mean limiting yourself to your lived experience, what does it mean? To me, it means that everything you have ever done, said, read, watched, learned, or imagined can inform and shape your writing. Beyond that, even if you don't know much about what you want to write, you can learn about it and then write about it.

To write what you know, you first have to know what you want to write. We covered that in the last section. If you're writing fiction set in the real world, even if you're writing about something that's very familiar to you, you will probably need to do at least some research to make sure you have your facts correct. The best fiction makes the imaginary seem real.

I believe one of the most effective ways to do this is to ground your fiction with a few real, tangible, believable facts. Suspension of belief is often necessary for readers, particularly in certain genres of fiction, but don't make it too hard for your readers to get there, and stay there. If you present false information as historical or scientific fact, your readers might reject your entire story. You can invent anything you want in order to tell your story, but try to avoid altering accepted facts. I can enjoy books that contradict my worldview as long as they don't contradict truth. Don't let this scare you out out of creativity, just do your homework. Get your facts checked. Don't try to spin the truth in order to support your agenda. Be a responsible writer. Truth is often found in fiction. I have learned volumes about a variety of subjects simply by reading well-researched fiction. A story that reads like a textbook can be very boring, but if you enrich your story with solid, relevant bits of information about a topic, career field, or historical period, it gives another layer of reality and believability to your plot and characters.

If you're writing speculative fiction, instead of research, you can focus your pre-writing efforts on world-building. This is why I love writing fantasy. I can let my wild imagination run free, creating entire worlds from nothing. "Write what you know" instead becomes, "Write whatever you make up." Still, even in this fanciful, imaginative style of storytelling, it's important to keep it grounded with natural laws and cultural norms for the world you create. Again, it's not necessary to focus too much on those things in the actual draft of your story. I personally find too much politics in a fantasy novel to be unpleasant and boring. Weave details in so that they move scenes forward, but don't leave your readers feeling like they are looking through binoculars at just your characters and plot, without seeing any of the world around them. Setting and backstory should stay in the background where they belong, but without them your story will feel incomplete.

Writing what you know means writing from both your learned knowledge and personal experience. Those are things that lend a particular flavor to your writing that can make it stand out. No one else knows the exact things you know, or has been through the life you've lived. There may be knowledge and experiences you can share that will resonate with others and make your plot feel solid and your characters seem relatable, while adding your personal touch to make the story live on in hearts long after the book is closed.

The best way to learn to write is to write. The best way to figure out what to write is to write. Are you sensing what I'm getting at here? Just write. Make it true to yourself, true to your worldview, true to the world around you, true in whatever version of reality you're writing. Good stories always embody some truth, so write truth the way you understand it.

Take Action:
- **List some things you know. Brainstorm about how you can write about those things.**
- **Also list some things you can learn that will enhance your writing.**
- **Write at least 500 words.**

EXPLORE NEW WORLDS

I am an information junkie. I love learning new things that I can add to my repertoire of what I jokingly call useless facts. If

I'm not careful, I can spend hours chasing trails on the internet or in a library, soaking up information like a sponge. I have two degrees, not so much because I love school or wanted to pursue a particular career, but because I enjoy learning. I also have a great imagination that can very quickly take me away from my normal life into all kinds of places and experiences. Exploring new worlds through reading and writing is one of my favorite things to do.

There have been a few times in my life where I had the unique experience of sitting around and talking with a group of authors. These people know a lot about a lot of things, often really random, unexpected things. Sometimes they can be rather gruesome and macabre. I've joked several times that authors usually know more ways to kill a person than a serial killer does. In researching and writing a book, authors can so fully immerse themselves in a particular topic or activity that they become experts. Then they move on to the next topic. It's a fascinating journey, and if you can get an author to talk about it, you might learn something.

Take some time to explore. You can do this by getting out of your house, out of town, venturing out and learning about the world by experiencing it. You can also do this without ever leaving your favorite spot by reading, surfing the internet, or just brainstorming images and concepts that come from your own mind.

One of the reasons why I love writing in coffee shops is because I can drift in and out of the real world, finding inspiration in interesting faces, music, scents, and even other customers' conversations. I am a shameless eavesdropper. I love people watching, and I also listen. If you sit near a writer

WRITING WHAT YOU KNOW MEANS WRITING FROM BOTH YOUR LEARNED KNOWLEDGE AND PERSONAL EXPERIENCE.

in a coffee shop, snippets of your conversations just might end up in a book. You never know. The world is full of inspiration. Be an observer. Every experience you have can add depth to your writing and give it a unique tone that no one else might have. Don't let those experiences go to waste. Pay attention.

If you know your story is missing something, but you can't place what that might be, I challenge you to sit down with your notebook or your computer and challenge yourself to come up with possible scenarios. In this situation, nothing is too outlandish. Write down everything that comes to your mind. One of my writer friends, Heather McCorkle, suggests interviewing your characters to find their motivation or to figure out what needs to happen next. I admit, I thought this was a silly idea until I tried it.

I was having a hard time writing my villain in a particular project. He was completely evil, not complex at all, and I couldn't figure out his reason for a certain set of actions I'd written for him. He just felt flat. So I wrote out an interview and basically asked, "Okay Mr. Villain, what's your deal?" I was surprised by all the words that flowed from my pen. After an hour or so of writing, I had a page or two full of things that I had never thought about this person before I tried asking him. Of course it was all coming from my own imagination, but the different approach was so helpful that I became an instant fan.

Interview your characters. Take a tour of your setting, a real world tour if possible, but at least in your mind. Write what you see, hear, smell, and experience. Write a scene from a different character's perspective. Discover how that character views your world and characters.

My favorite books are the ones that take me to a different time or place and immerse me so thoroughly in that world that I become a part of it. I want to write books that do that for others. To make your world real to other people, you must first make it real to you. The bulk of the work of world building and character development you do may never make it onto a published page, but you need to spend an adequate amount of time doing it. If not, your readers will know.

When I think of this topic I often think of *The Night Circus* by Erin Morgenstern. When I read some books, they paint such vivid pictures that I feel like I'm watching a movie. With that book though, I was there, part of the experience, smelling the food (chocolate popcorn!) and living the magic and tension of the story. Some books leave me with only an image or two and I wonder what happened in the rest of the book. Sometimes I don't even know what the characters look like. In my mind they're these creepy blank faces, and I can't feel a connection with that. Other books fill my mind with so many images and feelings that they become a part of my life. The characters are people I know. The places are so concrete in my mind, it's like I've been there. Those are my favorite books.

You can apply this concept to nonfiction too. Good writing introduces your readers to new concepts that they wouldn't necessarily know about otherwise. That's why people read. Know your topic, find new perspectives and new information you might not have considered before, and then share it. Share it in a way that readers can connect with and experience it for themselves. I rarely read nonfiction, but the books that I read all the way through are the ones that give me the best lasting images.

Explore new worlds. Take your readers along for the trip. Enjoy.

Take action:
- **Write a description of the place where you are right now. Make it at least 500 words. Use as much imagery and invoke as many senses as possible.**
- **Then share it with someone and ask if it feels real.**
- **Find out what might be missing.**

For the next week, pay attention to the people and places around you. Without being distracted and distant from anyone you might be with, look for inspiration for stories. It could be a couple at a restaurant, a bird at the window, a cloud in the sky, or an excellent meal. Anything that catches your attention and imagination is story fodder. Think about how you can use it.

EXPLORE
NEW WORLDS.
TAKE YOUR
READERS
ALONG FOR
THE TRIP.

· WRITE WELL

"The difference between the almost right word and the right word is really a large matter. 'Tis the difference between the lightning bug and the lightning."

— Mark Twain

LEARN YOUR CRAFT

Not everyone is a good writer, but I believe anyone can learn to write. If you are going to write, you owe it to yourself and your audience to write as well as you possibly can. I hope that by now you've established a habit of writing. Now let's look at some ways that we can all grow our skills in this area.

First, read. I am a firm believer that one of the best practices for writers is reading. There was a time in my life when I knew I wanted to be a writer, but I wasn't spending much time writing. Someone asked me if I was worried about that, because they figured writing ability was a "use it or lose it" kind of thing. I replied that as long as I keep reading, I'll always be able to write. When you read traditionally published work, you are reading what the top percentage of authors have written. I think that's some pretty good training material.

If you've never been much of a reader, become one. It's always easiest to read what interests you, whether that is a certain style of fiction, a particular author, a biography of someone you admire, or a topic that you want to learn more about. Once you've narrowed down your to-be-read (TBR) list, start reading. Great books always inspire me to write, and not-so-great books inspire me to help people write better.

You don't have to intentionally analyze every book you read, noting the plot structure and sentence construction. I admit, I do it. I'm a writing snob. I just can't help it. My favorite books are the ones that are so well-written that I don't notice the writing. If I get caught up in finding errors while I'm reading, I'm probably not reading a very good book.

While reading generally is a good way to learn to write, you can also read some of the many excellent writing craft books that are available. My personal favorite is a slim volume called *The Elements of Style* by Strunk and White. I highly recommend it to anyone who wants to improve their writing. It is concise, pithy, and timeless. If you enjoy that, you can also get a reference copy of *The Chicago Manual of Style*, which I must admit I occasionally read for fun. I am a grammar geek, and the Chicago Manual is full of helpful, sometimes witty, technical advice. The size is daunting but it includes a helpful index. I've read a few other craft books, including books on plot, structure, and world-building. A quick search on the internet or in your local library will lead you to some good ones.

The internet is a nearly limitless source of writing craft resources. Some of my personal favorites are the Books & Such Blog, Writers Helping Writers, K. M. Weiland's site, and the Steve Laube Agency blog. There are many, many others. Online, you can access courses, videos, tutorials, and articles on any writerly subject you can imagine. Writers love to write, and many of them love to write about writing, myself included. The internet is constantly changing, but if you need guidance for where to start, I keep a list of my favorite resources on my blog.

Conferences provide another excellent opportunity to learn about writing. I have only attended a few small ones, but the focused learning and the connection with other writers made them completely worth the time and money. Some of the best, most practical pieces of writing advice I've ever heard came from a conference or writer retreat.

Speakers are successful writers who know their craft and their trade, and the chance to sit at the feet of these masters is invaluable. Fellow attendees make fascinating conversation partners, once you get past the awkward introduction stage. Most writers tend to be introverts, but once you get them talking, the words flow freely through a variety of topics.

Beyond the opportunities for learning and social connection, conferences also offer ways to get your writing in front of people who can help you polish and eventually publish it. They can be expensive and often require travel, but if you are able to attend at least one every year or two, I think you'll be glad you did.

EDIT YOURSELF

As a proofreader and editor, I can say with confidence that if you learn to edit your work well, editors will love you. Don't be tempted to think, "But editing is their job, not mine." Writers who need very little correction are a joy to work with. I've edited beautifully written material and material that I look at several times, scratch my head, and think, "What are they even saying here?" Trust me, the writers who write well and offer drafts that are mostly error-free are the most enjoyable.

I've noticed that when it comes to self-editing, there seem to be two different camps of writers. First there are those who edit as they write, laboring over each word and sentence, making sure it says precisely what they want it to before moving on. These people might take a long time to craft a first draft, but once it is finished, it's very clean and well-written, requiring few rewrites and editorial input before moving on to the next step in the writing process. Then there are those who are able to shut off their "internal editor" while writing a fast first draft, just letting the words flow. They then go back and edit several times before passing their work off to a professional editor. Both of these methods are perfectly acceptable.

You can adopt either, or land somewhere in the middle like I do, and still end up with a very nice draft. It just depends on whether you'd rather put in the work on word crafting and editing in your first draft or subsequent drafts. Both methods ultimately require a similar amount of time and effort. Pick the one that works best with your personality, and get to writing and editing. There is no shame in writing an imperfect first draft, as long as no one else has to read it.

Personally, my method is to write whatever comes to mind first, and then go back and clean it up later. Sometimes I also edit as I go. I have a habit of tacking sentences on to the end of paragraphs and then realizing they will work better early on, so I move them. I also insert thoughts into my paragraphs wherever I think they fit best. If I have to leave off in the middle of a thought, scene, or chapter, I will read over what I already wrote when I come back to it. I often do some touch-up editing at that point, fixing places where I typed the wrong word or left a word out, or clarifying a thought or sentence with better wording.

Generally, I prefer to write an entire draft before going back to edit. This gives me an opportunity to look at the work with fresh eyes and see ways to improve it. Reading the same words over and over can cause mental fatigue and blindness to the problems in a manuscript. If you feel that happening in a particular chapter or passage, take a break, work on something else, and then come back to it.

I suggest making several editorial "passes" over your work before an editor looks at it. First, look for obvious typographical and grammatical errors. Next, evaluate the readability and flow. This is a great time to read your work out loud, or if you can't bring yourself to do that, have a software program read it for you. Sometimes a sentence sounds perfectly acceptable in your head, but it doesn't work when you read it out loud. Fix that. Take another pass, and read it over for content.

If you're writing fiction, consider character arcs, plot points, and pacing. Does every scene move the plot forward or add to character development? Bonus points if it does both, because every scene should. If not, you can either cut it or add essential elements to it. Some scenes may be in the wrong place entirely. Move them around, and then edit again for flow. If you're writing nonfiction, pacing is still important.

Make sure your structure is sound. Sometimes when I'm doing informative or reflective writing, it's easy to let my thoughts run on and stray from the point. When I'm editing I can clean that up and make sure I stay on topic.

If you did not use an outline in your original draft, create one based on what you wrote, and make sure your thoughts are in order and easy to follow. Finally, read the entire manuscript one more time and touch up anything you might have missed. Once all that is done and you feel good about your work, it's ready for an editor.

Does that sound like a lot of work? Good, because it is. Writing words that people will enjoy reading is a long and difficult process. If you truly love writing, you will enjoy most of the process. You might hate parts of it, but you are doing good work, pouring yourself into something that others will one day appreciate. I can guarantee that editors will appreciate your hard work as well. You want to make their job easy for two reasons: They will like you more, and it will cost less. Hiring an editor is expensive, whether you do it yourself or a publisher does it for you. If you do the work up front, it will make everyone happier. If they have to spend hours rewriting your work because you didn't take the time to do it, you may not like the result. If you can establish a good relationship with an editor who enjoys working with you and understands your voice and vision, everyone wins.

Take action:
- **Edit yourself! Look at a piece of writing you've done and follow the steps outlined above.**
- **Ask a grammar nazi or writer friend to read your work after you've edited it, and ask for suggestions on how you could improve your self-editing.**

GET FEEDBACK

You've developed a habit of writing. You've taken your writing public in some arena. You've polished your work until it's as good as you can make it. Now what? Time to take it a step further and get some critical eyes on what you've written. Gulp.

I thrive on feedback. Words of affirmation and praise are extremely important to me, but I also value critical suggestions. I'm so interested in feedback that I let a few people read my work before I'm even finished with it, to find out if it's hitting the right emotional tones and flowing the way I want it to. I ask for more feedback on the completed project and any subsequent rewrites. I even have a few people that I ask to read my blog posts after I publish them but before I promote them.

Sometimes what I write sounds brilliant to me, but when someone else reads it, they point out that it has a tone I didn't intend or lacks clarity in certain areas. In the case of my first completed novel, I found out that the stakes weren't high enough for my main character. That's when I realized I needed to go back to the drawing board and work on my plot. Other times I get a thrill when people tell me that they were moved by a particular scene or inspired by a thought. Getting feedback on your writing can be painful, but occasionally it can remind you of why you write and motivate you to keep going.

> Getting feedback on your writing can be painful, but occasionally it can remind you of why you write and motivate you to keep going.

In looking for feedback, I suggest asking at least three people: a friend or family member; someone who's knowledgeable about your topic or genre or at least interested in it; and a neutral person who knows writing and will give an honest opinion. If you can get feedback from several people, you'll have a better idea of how your writing will impact your audience than if you get an opinion from just one. By this point you may have a writing community that you can approach. Perhaps you could offer to trade critiques.

When I ask for feedback, I like to have a list of questions ready to help my readers as they think through what they're reading. Sometimes I save the questions until after they've read through it once, so I can ask for their impressions without feeling like I've led them, and other times I ask them to keep the questions in mind as they read. That depends on the sort of feedback I'm looking for. Some of my typical questions are:

- Did you enjoy what you read? What did you like most about it? What did you like least?
- How would you summarize the main theme/plot points?
- If fiction: Which characters were your favorite? Why?
- What did you think of the pacing of the plot or flow of ideas?
- Do you have any suggestions for how I could improve this?

I don't like to overwhelm people with questions, but I do like to guide their feedback a little bit so that it's useful for me as I seek to improve my writing. While I love hearing, "It's great! Don't change a thing!" I'd rather hear that about the finished project than a work in progress that still needs polishing. The people I consistently ask for feedback are the ones who honestly evaluate my work and challenge me to do better.

If someone asks you for feedback, I suggest proceeding with caution. I'm always happy to look at what someone has written, so much so that I offer it as a paid service. I want to help people write better, and I enjoy looking at what someone else has created. I praise what I like about it and offer suggestions for what could be improved, as well as asking questions that I'd like to see answered in the work.

I believe the best method for a critique is the sandwich method. Start out praising what you liked about what you read. Be specific, pulling out a quote or noting how you could relate to a character or event. Next, address the problems. Do this tactfully and as gently as possible, knowing that creatives often have easily bruised egos. Finally, end with a compliment of the entire work, perhaps that you like the author's voice, or the plot was engaging, or the writing was excellent and almost error-free.

In a friendly (or even a paid) critique, please avoid the possible temptation to rip someone's work to shreds. There is a strong tendency to do this, especially in Amazon or Goodreads reviews, and in some writer forums. People these days think they are the world's greatest critics, and the ability to point out every flaw in a book or story is a matter of pride. Before getting carried away with a cleverly worded, harsh review in any environment, stop and think how you would feel if you were that author, and you had to read those words about what you've written. It can be painful and extremely discouraging. As part of a writing exercise, I once asked an acquaintance to read through the first 20 pages of my novel and point out any spots where she would stop reading. What I got back was a thorough critical evaluation that was so stinging, I completely lost my confidence and momentum in that story. I needed to know some of what was said, but the way it was said was hurtful and it made me angry. Don't to that to your friends, or no one will ask you to read their writing again.

When you ask someone else for their opinion of your writing, be prepared for anything. You never know how someone will respond to what you've written. I hope that what you hear back will be positive and encouraging, but even if it's harsh and critical, you can learn from that and improve. Negative feedback doesn't mean you've failed as a writer. Even the best writers get bad reviews. Learn to take the good with the bad, learn as much as you can, and be the best writer you can be.

Take action:
- **Have three different people evaluate a piece of writing and give you feedback.**
- **Summarize the responses and think through ways you can improve your writing.**
- **If possible, ask the same people to read the next draft and tell you what they think.**

• WRITE LIKE A NINJA

"I may not look like much,

but I'm an expert at

pretending to be a ninja."

— *Darynda Jones, First Grave on the Right*

WRITING IS A JOURNEY — PRACTICE PATIENCE

I've been a part of the #WritersRoad chat on Twitter for several years. Once a month we tweet writing advice and inspiration. One silly piece of advice we often come back to is: When your story is lagging or you need to add some action, do something surprising. Catch your readers off guard. Increase the stakes. Add a spark of danger. Create an explosion ... or add ninjas. Erin Morgenstern credits the "just add ninjas" philosophy to NaNoWriMo wisdom but I haven't found the actual source. It doesn't matter to me where it came from. I think it's great.

I've taken it as a personal challenge to add ninjas (note: the ninjas do not have to be *actual* ninjas ... but I figure they might as well be) to my writing whenever possible, whether it really works in the context or not. In the true spirit of #WritersRoad, I'm wrapping my writing advice by adding ninjas. Or at least some inspiration from the ninja life. I'm not a ninja. I've only seen them on movies and read about them on the internet. I have learned a few things about being a ninja that I want to apply to being a writer. If you want to write like a ninja, follow these principles:

First, practice patience. Ninjas train for years in their particular art, and they know to wait until the perfect moment to strike. Writing requires patience, too. I started writing stories when I learned to write words. I can remember writing my first unicorn story in Kindergarten. I have pursued other passions and careers in the decades since then, but writing has always been at the core of my being.

From the time I started writing, I knew I wanted to be a published author and share my words with the world. The original goal was to be published by age 10. When that didn't quite work out, I pushed it back to 15. By that time I realized I still had a lot to learn about writing, and a lot to do to hone my craft.

I'll be honest, for many years I did not put in the work I needed in order to really write well. I did keep reading, inventing stories, and dabbling in writing in my spare time. I have a blog now, so I do write in public, but I still haven't reached that point of being published. My 10-year-old self would stomp her foot and say I'm a failure. The way I see it now, I'm on a journey. I haven't reached my destination, but every stop along the way has been valuable.

I can practice patience.

You are who you are today because of your life experiences and the choices you have made. We might all have some similarities in our personalities, backgrounds, and circumstances, but we are all unique. No one has lived your life in the particular way you have. Every part of your life colors your writing in a palette of hues that belongs exclusively to you. I'm not suggesting that you should be pushing 40 before you attempt to publish a book, but if you are, or if you've left

40 long behind, you have not failed as a writer. Writing only improves with age.

I have touched on the patience required in this writing journey already, but I want to really emphasize it now. Learning to write, churning out words, enduring the often slow and painful process of selling your book, waiting for it to finally hit shelves, can all take a lot of time. I know authors who write and publish their books in six months or less. Some can draft a novel in a month or two. I also know the agony of waiting and waiting for a new book from authors who seem to take forever to release their latest work. Whether you write fast or slow, self-publish or are published traditionally, there is time involved. Keep working on your craft and your projects, but take the time you need to make it what you know it needs to be. Your readers will appreciate your efforts.

I do want to offer a word of caution. It may be possible to be too patient. If you never launch your writing into the world, no one will have a chance to read it. Don't get so caught up in waiting for the right moment to hit publish or submit or send that you miss your opportunity. Part of practicing patience is knowing when to make your move, and then actually making it.

Take action:
- **Practice patience.**
- **Enjoy the journey.**
- **Write some words.**

KNOW WHEN TO ADJUST — FREEDOM AND FLEXIBILITY

Ninjas know that sometimes it's important to adjust their plan of action or fighting style in response to their enemies' actions. While I hope you're not fighting an enemy (although your characters might be), I think we can apply this principle in terms of being fluid and flexible. Don't box yourself in to a certain style, tone, or even place and time where you write. We talked earlier about being willing to take detours in your writing. Sometimes it's okay for your life to take a detour, too. If something isn't working for you, change it. If you want to try something new, go for it. If opportunities aren't coming to you, go out and look for them.

Or create them for yourself. In this age of new media and the internet, there are endless opportunities for a writer wanting to get exposure or even get hired. You don't even have to wait for a publisher to accept you if you don't want to. You can publish your book yourself. For some writers, that might be the right move. For others, getting out to conferences or taking on freelance gigs might be better. Do what you need to do.

I think there are a few misconceptions about writers out there. There's this idea that writing books is like prospecting for gold, that once you've "made it," you're rich and successful. Another idea is the picture of the "starving artist," who writes all the time and never gets paid. Both of these are inaccurate representations of reality.

IF THE ONLY CONSTANT IN LIFE IS CHANGE, YOU NEED TO BE ABLE TO GO WITH THE FLOW IN ORDER TO ADAPT AND SUCCEED.

While there are a few authors among the rich and famous, most writers, including those who have written bestsellers, make only a modest living. However, it *is possible* to make a living as an author. As author and blogger Jeff Goins says, you don't have to be a starving artist. This is essentially self-employment in a small business. You can make a lot of money or a little, depending on how much and how consistently you work and take advantage of the opportunities that are available. You have the freedom to choose to make this your full-time career and the flexibility to work the way that works for you. Most writers have a full-time or part-time job or volunteer gig (like parenting) and write on the side. You may be content with that, or you may want more. It's up to you.

There may be times in your writing life when you have more freedom and some times when you have less. Professional writers have deadlines, expectations and assignments from editors and publishers, and an often-critical audience of readers to please. If you haven't reached that point yet, you do have a lot of freedom to write what you want when you want to. Even if you are under contract or on assignment, you still get to decide when and where and how you're going to get those words out. If the only constant in life is change, you need to be able to go with the flow in order to adapt and succeed.

Take action:
- **Choose what kind of writer you want to be: full-time, part-time, or spare time.**
- **Plan and work accordingly.**
- **Evaluate where you are now and how happy you are with your current situation, and make necessary adjustments.**
- **Write some words.**

ALWAYS KEEP THEM GUESSING — SNEAKY SURPRISES

Ninjas are best known for their sneak attacks. They hide patiently, sometimes in plain sight, for that moment when their targets feel safe. Then they move in, suddenly and unexpectedly, and press their advantage. The most effective attack is often the one you didn't see coming. This is just as true in writing — especially fiction — as it is in martial arts.

Your readers are not your enemies, and I'm not suggesting that you attempt to harm them with your sneaky surprises. I am suggesting that the best plot twists are the ones that are set up so well that you didn't see them coming, but once they are revealed you realize they should have been obvious all along.

I have read a lot of books. I am familiar with many varieties of tropes, and I am pretty adept at separating red herrings from true plot clues and accurately predicting how a book will end. There are few authors so brilliant that they manage to both surprise and delight me with "sneak attack" plot twists, and I always appreciate it when they do. Laini Taylor is a master of this. In particular, her books *A Daughter of Smoke and Bone* and *Strange the Dreamer* blew me away. I can honestly say I don't know how she does it, other than genius and hard work.

The books I appreciate most are the ones that follow a universal theme or plot arc closely enough that I can comfortably say, "I know where this is going," but that toss in a few truly surprising elements that keep me both satisfied and engaged with the story. This is a delicate balance that requires ninja-like training, patience, and focus. If your big reveal turns out to be a big yawn, you'll lose readers. Similarly, if your big reveal comes so completely out of left field that you leave readers confused and frustrated, you'll lose them there, too. If you're so afraid to lose readers that you keep your story pedantic and predictable, guess what? That's right. You'll lose readers. No one will want to read your books.

The key is to offer hints about what's coming without completely giving it away. You also want to avoid insulting your readers by obviously refusing to give them key information. I think of this like dangling a carrot in front of a mule. The mule wants the carrot, he knows it's there, but he can't quite reach it, so he keeps moving forward. Don't treat your readers like stubborn mules. Engage them with your story and in your characters so that they keep reading because they want to know what's going to happen next, not because they're promised some big "aha" moment approximately 75-85% into the story.

You can work sneaky surprises into nonfiction too, but it's a more subtle art. While staying consistent within your platform, you can bring in interesting tidbits, personal stories, illustrations about famous people or events, and a touch of humor to break up the monotony and lighten the tone. People read nonfiction because they want to be informed or educated, but there is still a touch of entertainment value in it, too. These days, information is available everywhere from Netflix to Wikipedia to the checkout stand at the grocery store. Intrigue readers with your own personal flair so that they pick your work and recommend it to friends, and you'll always have an audience.

Take action:
- **Think of stories (books or movies) that effectively surprised you with a mind-blowing plot twist.**
- **Why was it so surprising? How did it make you feel?**
- **Come up with two or three plot ideas and imagine several sneaky surprises you could add to keep the story moving.**
- **Congratulate yourself for finishing this book.**
- **Write something!**

ACKNOWLEDGMENTS

No book worth reading is the work of only one person. I have so many people to thank for helping make this happen. My editor, Lisa Voth was a godsend. I appreciate your quick work and insight. My designer, Kristen McGregor, is a delight to work with. Your talent, work ethic, and personality are fantastic! Thanks to my behind-the-scenes support team, Ashley Linne, Chris Kochis, Krissi Dallas, Maria Gauna, and many others who have given me advice and feedback. Heather McCorkle, your friendship and encouragement has meant so much to me over the years. I hope we get to meet in person someday! To my friends, cohorts, and instructors in the Work-At-Home School, especially Caitlyn Pyle, Talia Browne, Colleen Mitchell, Maria McGinnis, Emma Bates, and Ashley Gainer, thank you for your helpful courses, ideas, and encouragement. Thanks to my mom and dad, Karen and John Zondlo, who have always been my biggest supporters. And of course to my loyal husband Greg, who faithfully goes along with whatever crazy idea I come up with next, and my sweet silly kids, Katelyn and Nathan, who love to read and want to make books like Mommy. I couldn't have done all of this without all of you!

www.ingramcontent.com/pod-product-compliance
Lightning Source LLC
Chambersburg PA
CBHW020301030426
42336CB00010B/860